W9-CLA-102

#single

#single

Dating in the 21st Century

LOST
THE
PLOT

LOST
THE
PLOT

A Lost the Plot Book. First published in 2017 by Pantera Press Pty Limited
www.PanteraPress.com

Design and typography copyright © Pantera Press Pty Limited, 2017

Please send all permission queries to:
Pantera Press, P.O. Box 1989 Neutral Bay, NSW 2089 Australia or info@PanteraPress.com

A Cataloguing-in-Publication entry for this book is available from the
National Library of Australia.

ISBN 978-1-921997-99-0 (Hardback)
Cover and Internal Design: Anthony Skujins
Typesetting: Kirby Jones

Dating in the 21st century is *rough*

"The perfect book to shove in the face of anyone who has ever asked 'Why are you still single?'"

My Next Door Neighbour, Fran

"Definitely giving this to all my friends who have (or, are) suffering through online dating"

Everyone I've Ever Met

Grammar

Wow, your beautiful!

No. You're beautiful

Awww

But, don't you mean handsome?

No... I was just correcting your grammar

#HB

What a beautiful name!

Thanks, I got it for my birthday

Huh?

Laugh Out Loud

LOL

You have a beautiful laugh

What?

Incorrect

Can I take you out for coffee this week?

That's not how you spell beer

A Picture
Is Worth
1000 Words,
Sometimes

If you looked up the word "beautiful" in the dictionary, there would be a photo of you! :)

That's unusual

What, you can't take a compliment?

No, I meant the dictionary isn't generally a picture book

Romance

I wanna do you slowly

Ain't nobody got time for that

Truth be told, I only need a minute or 2 max

Hello?

Apply Cold Water To Burn

Words can't even begin to describe how beautiful you are

Ditto... Words can't describe how handsome you are

:)

But numbers can

3/10

Unsubscribe
Here

I think it's good to keep breakups short, simple and clean. But high maintenance girls always seem to get offended when I text them 'unsubscribe'

Unsubscribe

Hahaha

The person you are texting has unsubscribed. We apologise for any inconvenience. You will be charged for this text

You're serious?

Ok, I guess this does actually hurt a bit...

But My Mum Says I'm Cool

I passed out by 9 last night :)

Word!

Nine

Yep… I got that

Uncultured

I thought you were worldlier. I can't be with someone so uncultured. I'm sure you understand. Best of luck with you're future endeavours

Your*

OUCH

Hey :)

Hey, survived the weekend?

You are SUPER adorable!

Ha. Thank you!

Sorry

Wrong person!

Subtext

Do you want to see a pic of my duck?

Yes

Dick*

No

Accidental Confession

Why do girls always cry during sex?

Mmmm Farts

Weird question... but do you fart much?

I find it a huge turn on...

Eggplant
Emoji

Talk dirty to me!

Unlaundered gym socks

What? Haha. No, say something hot!

Jaffle Maker

Is that a sex toy?

In The Wise Words Of
Words Of
Disney

In the wise words of Sebastian the Crab... "Darling it's better, down where it's wetter. Take it from me" ;)

Freudian Slip

I can show you the world. Shining, shimmering, splendid...

Tell me prisoner, now when did you last let your heart decide?

In Vino Veritas

So, dinner Thursday?

Let me drink about it

Think* :)

No, I meant what I said!

GenY

Do you want to talk on the phone?

No

Why not?

Because I'm Gen Y

So you have a problem with your phone?

My only problem with my phone is that I can't delete the 'phone' app on it

I meant, do you have a problem talking on the phone?

Clearly

Damn You
Autocorrect

Sounds good. Lesbian shortly, just one more drink!

LEAVING* shortly

Arrive Alive – Don't Text & Drive

Hey gurl, this is super corny to say but when I see your profile it makes me smile. You just seem so contagiously happy. Fuck you you mother fucker cont what the fuck? Are you fucking kidding? You stupid shit of a person I'll fucking kill you. Oh crap, stop

... Well this is awkward. Apologies... I was using "speech to text" to message you and someone cut me off while I was driving

All You Need
Is Wit

How r u?

Wen can we meet?

Hey

So, drinks?

You're not pretty enough to be this bad at conversations

So, drinks?

Acronym Fail

I should be upfront, I have DS

?

Most people say they wouldn't have suspected it, so I thought I should be honest

Is that a deal breaker for you?

I hope not. It's just me most of the time, except for every 3 weeks

You have DS every 3 weeks??

Yes, and some holidays

... I'm assuming DS does not stand for Down Syndrome in this instance?

DARLING SON!!! OMG, is that what people think DS means?

... Well that explains a lot...

Adulting

Let's party this weekend?

I love parties! Will there be party hats and lolly bags?

Umm no?

Sounds like a dud party. What about a magician? Will there be a magician?

What?

What I meant was, do you want to play this weekend?

Ohhhhh. Why didn't you just say so?

;)

Play dates are my thing! Sandpits and juice boxes, can't go wrong. I make a mean sandcastle!

What?

How old are you?

29 and three quarters

Right

You know what I mean, right?

Yes

;) ;) ;)

I was just saying yes to be cool

Do you want to hook up this weekend?

Ohhhhh why didn't you just say so!

:)

No

Huh

No, my answer is no

Not A Death Threat

I can't wait to meet you dead girl

Ummm dear* I meant dear girl...

How To Host
A Murder

3 uses for a blanket... go:

1. Warmth while sleeping
2. Structural walls in pillow fort building
3. To hide bodies of bad Tinder dates

Stranger
Danger

15 years together, and we broke up a little over a year ago. So I'm quite new to the modern dating scene

Tell me more about this 'modern' dating scene

Well for starters, in my day you didn't meet people from the Internet in real life... or get in strangers cars for that matter. And these days, you literally summon strangers from the Internet with the purpose of getting in their car

Honesty Is
The Best
Policy

I have an amazing penis, and an average personality

It's Not
Romance
That's Dead

How are you still single?

Sometimes I go too far with erotic asphyxiation and well... let's just say partners don't last long

See My Vest

What's your favourite flower?

I kinda like Orchids. What about you?

Oh, I hate flowers. I just wanted to know what to put on your grave when I murder you

Oh cute! Forward thinking, I like your style

Well I can't exactly ask you afterwards, can I?

Guess not. I will just say, you're going to need to buy me dinner first

Ok. But only if I get to wear your skin afterwards

If You're Happy & You Know It... Clap Your Hands

Matching with you is my biggest regret

Getting gonorrhoea is mine

So you have the clap?

When you spread it around… is it called applause?

…

I guess STI jokes are only funny when you don't have any

Wait, you're not a cyber bot?

Correct

You're a real person?

Realer than Pinocchio

Shit

No Take Backsies

You're a stupid bitch. I wouldn't have sex with you any way

... Want to have sex?

#SorryNotSorry

I just found your profile on Instagram... and you're way less attractive than I anticipated. But, good chat – all the best with work

Smile

Your beautiful smile lights up a room!

Thanks. I coat my teeth twice daily in UV liquid from the inside of purple glow sticks

What?

It works much better than Colgate whitening tooth paste

Huh?

For my teeth!

to light up the room!

Isn't that poisonous?

Well... Yes. I have 3 months to live. But it was worth it for all the compliments I get online about my smile :)

So... you're just looking for a one-night stand?

Never Underestimate Originality... Except In This Case

Hey, you look lovely and have a great figure from what looks like super amazing nutrition!! Fancy meeting up sometime for some family friendly fun?

Grippy Tannins With A Hint Of Manure

Did you know that after you smell something for 20 seconds you can no longer smell it. Which is why at wine tastings they give you coffee beans to sniff in between smelling the wines... to break up the scent experience

After I take a poo, I often run back into the bathroom to smell how toxic it was

Party of 1

Hey

Want to go for a drink tonight?

That sounds good :) When can y do?

Did you just respond to your own drink invitation?

Yeh. My bad. LOL

For A Good Time, Call...

Let's meet up for a good time

Define "good time"

Hot sex with a handsome stranger

Oh cool. What's he look like? Will you introduce me to him?

Not funny

No?

Delete

Not A
Serial Killer

Hey there, how are you? I was really hoping we'd match!!

You know my father always told me to base my opinion of a woman on her smile... and (as tacky as this may sound) you have a gorgeous smile...

So I have a proposal to make (as forward as this might sound) I think we should exchange phone numbers so I can call you, charm you with my intellect and wit and ask you out to dinner... so we can finally get the hell off Tinder... sounds like a solid plan to me!

Well Sam*, you make a strong argument... but I'm going to need to know a little more...

Tell me the top 3 most important things I need to know about you, that prove you're not a serial killer ;)

My ego and pride are so much so that I'd never risk going to jail or losing my freedom!

Killing someone or raping them is absolutely NOT challenging at all, so it doesn't appeal to me

And lastly, check me out!! I'm too 'topless selfie' to be a modern-day Ted Bundy... my eyes are too innocent!! It's all in the eyes!!!

Hello?

Hello?

Seriously??

Excuse me??? You ask a question, I responded and you don't get back to me… generally if I ask a question, I wait around for the answer… it's courteous

Clearly you've got lots of baggage

If you're going to have that sorta shit attitude, you're more than welcome to unmatch me, Oprah!

Persistence & Stalking: The Key To Any Relationship

Hey

Hey

Hey

I hope you don't mind my frankness! But thanks to the wonders of modern technology I've discovered a bit about you and your impressive career, and you seem intriguing

Drinks?

I now appreciate that might seem creepy

Hey

Catch Of
The Day

Hello again

Hi

Hello beautiful

Hello? Why are you ignoring me?

I drive a Porsche!

#Charming

#charming   9.04pm

Hey

Stupid Slut. Enjoy the cock carousel

Standard

What are you up to today?

Beating my meat, thinking about you

#BadDay

Not too bad. Recovering from a big weekend, but no complaints. You?

Fuck you and your happy life

Kiss Me Through The Phone

I have chlamydia :) You should get tested

Wait, what?

What the fuck is wrong with you?

: (

How dare you ducking put my life in jeopardy like this! And my future chickens life

EIEIO

WHAT THE FUCK IS THAT

I thought we were singing nursery rhymes with the mentions of ducks and chickens?

NO WE ARE FUCKING NOT. You know what I meant. ARE YOU REALLY MAKING JOKES. YOU GAVE ME AN STI YOU PSYCHO

Think about it

I'm going to come after you

That's not very nice

I'm going to put your future children at risk too

That's very Rumpelstiltskin of you

YOU FUCKING WHORE

Ok, before we get too threat heavy... do you want to take a breather and remember that not only have we not slept together... But we've literally never even met...

I was just joking

Drinks this week?

Nah

Psycho

Wanted:
A Sweet,
Normal Girl

I haven't been on any actual Tinder dates yet. It's all a bit intimidating. Until now I've been yet to find the sweet normal girls!

So sweet, normal girl, what's on for you this weekend?

Is that so?

This weekend I've got a good friends birthday on Friday and then I have a bachelor party all day Saturday. Sunday I'm reserving for death and/or recovery. You?

I think you mean bachelorette party? ;)

Negatory. It's a bachelor party. One of my best mates is getting married. Prepping my liver as we speak :)

Oh that's so cool!

Like seriously cool!

So you're basically one of the guys, huh?

Does that mean you're into dildos and dildo shows and that kind of stuff :) :) :)

The Little
Train That
Could

Do you still want to meet up?

What's kept you so busy? Reach out!

Do you have plans tonight?

Never heard from you so I made other plans. Have a good one

Lets give next week a shot. See if you can fit me in

You're not a big communicator are ya? I'm having brunch with a friend at 9am tomorrow

Change of plans. I'm working for my dad; I should be back by 9.45am. Let me know to meet up!

I love to communicate. Especially when I'm just meeting someone I might be interested in. If you could let me know by 9? Thanks so much. The first month of dating can be brutal!

Brutally important*. I shouldn't be texting and driving!

I think I'm looking for more in a relationship. In the beginning I'm so excited. I want to learn everything about you. That's me! I'm just a happy intense guy that liked you. All the best

I have 1 question for you and I'll never bother you again. The only reason you don't want to see me is because of the texts? It wont hurt my feelings. It's got to be something more. The only reason I ask is I haven't met someone that I have so much in common with

Thought we have tentative plans for Saturday from our conversation on Thursday?

Anyway, sorry for blowing up your phone

Good evening. I apologise for the crazy texts.
Any way that you can give this guy another shot?
There's a lot more to see than you got to see

I'm guessing that's a no? You can't blame a guy for trying

Let me know if we can meet up

New Year's
Resolution #1

My new years resolution is to be the new Kim Kardashian

Kimmy K hey? That's an unusual one, for a man. What's the plan? Surgery?

A sex tape

Oh, I walked in to that one!

New Year's Resolution #2

Are you sticking to your New Years resolutions?

For sure. My "don't make love to a supermodel" resolution is going great so far!

New Year's
Resolution #3

I'm about to start a new job next week. So I guess my New Years resolution is to survive the week!

Good luck! What's the role?

Thanks. It's also a graphic designer role, but more senior. And what's your New Years resolution?

I'm not sure… Probably I'll keep it at around 300dpi

Tell That
To My Pet
Unicorn

In the Christmas spirit I have been tormenting my interns at work, I convinced one that reindeers are real ;)

Reindeers are real

Hahaha tell that to my pet unicorn

Reindeers. Are. Real.

Now you're just messing with me

Http://lmgtfy.com/?q=reindeer

Oh shit

I thought reindeer were Christmas myths like Santa and the North Pole

How do they fly?

In The 'Spirit'
Of Easter

What are you doing to celebrate Easter?

Getting hammered and nailed!

Happy Easter

Well it's only been a few weeks, but I have been seeing two girls. Both very low key situations, but I'm just trying not to put all my eggs in one basket

But it's Easter!

?

You should put all your eggs in one basket... as long as they are chocolate... and it's my basket ;)

Google Translate: British To Australian

Ello Guvna

HaHa. Why hello there

I'm from Australia. Just visitin' fer bottle ov glue weeks. Know what I mean?

No?

Awright geeezzaa! Thee don't know what I mean?

But I'm usin' me 'Australian ter English, transalator app

What?

Blimey, are yew not from England?

Born and bred London

Is English your second language?

No???

Don't you speak English in Australia?

No. We speak Australian, mate

Isn't that the same?

Obviously not

Oh sorry, I didn't realise. Are there big differences?

I'm using Google translate right now to decipher your messages

Is it really that different?

Absolutely

Wow. I met an Australian recently and they didn't let on at all. Although he looked a bit confused – maybe I should have spoken slower! Woops

Sandpaper wall flower on Sundays

What was that?

Google translate is the worst. Innit?

Are you really translating this conversation?

Can You Hear Me Now?

Hey Girl

HELLO :)

Did you have a good weekend?

YES IT WAS GREAT. I'M STILL RECOVERING ;) BUT IT WAS LOVELY NONETHELESS. YOU?

All caps makes it look like you're shouting ;)

I AM SHOUTING

Haha okay?

I'M HALF DEAF

Oh okay!

YEP

Wait, what?

I Heart Dates

Why is a date with me better than a date?

Do you mean a date with another person?
Or a date, as in the pitted fruit?

I meant with another person. But the fruit one will
make me sound even better, so let's do that one ;)

So the question is 'why is dating you better
than an actual date, the fruit'?

Yes

Well… I've weighed up the pros and cons

And unfortunately you didn't come out so great

I think a date would likely leave one more
satisfied and less sticky, than you would

Plus, dates are sweet

And, finally – I'd rather go on a picnic with dates
(they go well with prosciutto and cheese)

Sorry

… This took a very unexpected turn. I guess
I'm not the catch I thought I was

No hard feelings

Expert Advice

Helppppppp me!

Why? What's wrong?

I'm iron deficient

Are you a vegetarian?

No. But I don't see how that's relevant?

Well, if you're anaemic and you don't eat red meat that can be a contributing factor

But I'm not anaemic, I'm iron deficient

It's basically the same thing. Have you tried supplements?

Will they prevent me from burning my clothes?

Wait, what?

When I'm ironing...

You're talking about ironing clothes? Why the fuck did you ask me? I'm a doctor!

Your shirt looks crease free in your profile photos

Australia

I'm living in town while I study at Yale University.
How are you finding New Haven?

Beautiful – from what I've seen so far. But
I'm only just surviving the humidity! You?

Haha how did you make your message
upside down? That is pretty cool!

I'm from Australia

Cool. But how come you're writing upside down?

My phone is from Australia. Australia
is on the other side of the world

Haha. That's crazy

Yes

I keep turning my phone upside down
so I can read your messages

Everything is upside down in Australia

Seriously?

Sure. It's hard while I've been visiting New Haven
– I've even had to walk on my hands for a bit, just
to balance things out. I must look so weird!

That makes total sense when you think about it. I'd just never given it any thought before. Wow... how do you go for drinks and stuff? Do you have to eat upside down while you're here? :(

Do you really go to Yale?

Stroke My Kitty

Hey

Have you seen my cat?

...?

Am I walking into a bad pick up line?

No, my cat Ron. He's with me in my profile pic

Have you seen him?

Is he missing? Or are you just gloating about his fame on a cat food ad?

He went missing from near ▆▆▆▆ Street and ▆▆▆▆ Street on Friday night

He's my best friend

I thought I'd reach out to the Tinder community to try and find him

And meet some pretty ladies in the process

Good luck in your search for Ron/a human friend/a cat lady on tinder. I'd say odds are at least 1 out of 3

Ouch

Wait, what would the bad pick up line have been?

Oh, I don't know… something unoriginal about a missing cat and wanting to play with someone else's pussy instead?

Totally using it!

You're welcome

#Stalker

Morning!

Morning

Cute shirt

You look good today

What?

Hahaha you just looked around to see if you could spot me!

?? Are you for real?

Are you sure you're looking at the right person?

Yep! Hiiiii

But I'm in my house?

I know, it's a nice house

You're really at my house? How did you find it?

I am indeed. Come out and say hi!

How can you even see me?

I'm looking through your front window

Are you sure you have the right guy/house?

Yes

██████████ St, New Haven?

Did you really just give your address to some random creep on the internet?

So you're not at my house?

Lose Yourself
In The Music

Can we be real for a minute... can you tell me a bit about yourself?

1. I can rap every word of Eminem's Slim Shady
2. I'm not a serial killer

Are the two connected?

Not as far as I know. Just trying to paint a holistic picture of my personality for you.

...?

You don't like Eminem?

Bye

Crazy Cat ~~Ladies~~ Men

Lovely to see a familiar face on here!

?

We go to the same gym

No

I'm sure we do? On ████████ Street?

I meant no, I'm not dating someone from my gym

Don't shit where you sleep?

Exactly

What's the worst that could happen?

One time I went for drinks with someone from my gym

Let's call him Jeremy*

He spent the night talking about 'Sharon'

You know… "I'd love to take you for dinner next week. But not tonight… because I promised Sharon I'd be home for dinner"

Ah, married?

Worse

?

Sharon was his cat

WHAT?

Long story short, I had to quit my gym

To avoid Jeremy*?

Yes. Also, real names have been used in this story

Suppose it doesn't help if I tell you I don't have a cat?

Affirmative

The Truth Is Out There

I think we've matched before?

Quite possibly!

I'm sure we did! I'm not sure why we stopped talking?

Perhaps my interest in alien abduction got in the way?

You're interested in alien abduction too?

Sure

So have you had any abduction experiences yourself?

Do you want to meet for a drink after work this week?

#MIB

What do you do for work?

I hunt aliens

Like immigrants?

No, like space invaders

Aliens aren't real. At least not the 'invade earth' kind

Have you ever seen one?

Obviously not

Well, you're welcome!

The Fresh Queen Of Tinder

I'm single, live on my own, work in a financial business. I very much enjoy keeping fit and active! I love the gym, basketball and golf. Hopefully that is a good start to telling you about me

Great life story!

I'm a big basketball fan too

In fact I grew up in the states, basketball is a big deal there

I was born and raised in West Philadelphia

That is, until I got into a bit of strife during a ball game and my mum shipped me off to live with my aunty and uncle

Is that when you came to Australia?

#Muggle

Public speaking is hard.
Sometimes I wish I was a magician!

Tell me about you

When I lived with my Aunty and Uncle, they made me sleep in a broom closet under the stairs

For real? An actual broom closet?

Or just a small room?

No, a real broom closet

What? Did you call child authorities?

Do you still see your aunt and uncle now?

Thankfully I spent a lot of my childhood at boarding school. So I did have a good escape

Did you at least have your own room there?

No, but all good. I shared it with my mate Ron

They let you share a room with a boy?

What can I say? Boarding school was a pretty magical experience!

What school did you go to?

I can't tell you

?

Why not?

Muggle

Shine Bright Like The Shining

What made you swipe right?

My finger

You?

Your finger made you?

I thought you looked cute

What other decisions has your finger made?

REDRUM

Oh no, my finger is at is again

REDRUM

REDRUM

REDRUM

OH NO, IT'S TAKING OVER

REDRUM

Are you ok?

REDRUM

Weekend At Bernie's

I'm at the movies right now, and the old lady next to me has fallen asleep on my shoulder. Any hot tips?

That's awkward! Is she drooling on you?

Let me think about it!!

So how was your night?

I spent the night at the cinema

I know! Was the movie good?

I mean, I slept at the cinema

I was waiting and waiting for your hot tip on how to extract myself from the old lady, so I just stayed there

All. Night.

This is kind of your fault if you think about it

O really?

Yep

So how did you get away then, miss?

Well, it turns out she wasn't asleep. She was dead

…

She was very old

You're not kidding?

Are you ok?

So how did you realise what happened?
Was she with anyone?

Have you seen "Weekend at Bernie's"?

Yes...

That's my plan!

What?

I've got her at my house right now

I don't think your joking... think I should call the police?

You're*

Happy Dude

Killer smile! You look so cheeky and happy :)

Greeting friend!

Do you wish to look as happy as me?

Most definitely :)

Well, you've got the power inside you right now

:D

So use it!

Send $1 to:
"Happy Dude: 742 Evergreen Terrace, Springfield"

Don't delay. Eternal happiness is just a dollar away

If I send the dollar, will you go out for coffee with me?

What's the rest of your address?

45501, OH

Wait... do you not live in Sydney?

Tinder says you're only 3km away...

D'oh

Heroes In A
Half-Shell

Why are man hole covers round?

I don't know, why?

They are made to perfectly fit in the pizza

What?

They are round, like pizza – to make it easy to deliver the pizza down there

You know a man hole is like a hole in the ground that connects to the storm water drains and sewers and stuff, right?

Tell that to Michelangelo #homesweethome

Michelangelo?

The artist?

TMNT?

TMNT?

You're dead to me